Gymnastics Superstar
Simone Biles

by Jon M. Fishman

BUMBA BOOKS™

LERNER PUBLICATIONS ◆ MINNEAPOLIS

Note to Educators

Throughout this book, you'll find critical-thinking questions. These can be used to engage young readers in thinking critically about the topic and in using the text and photos to do so.

Lerner Publications Company
A division of Lerner Publishing Group, Inc.
241 First Avenue North
Minneapolis, MN 55401 USA

For reading levels and more information, look up this title at www.lernerbooks.com.

Library of Congress Cataloging-in-Publication Data

Names: Fishman, Jon M., author.
Title: Gymnastics superstar Simone Biles / by Jon M. Fishman.
Description: Minneapolis, Minnesota : Lerner Publications, [2019] | Series: Bumba Books | Audience: Ages: 4–7. | Audience: Grades: K to Grade 3. | Includes bibliographical references and index.
Identifiers: LCCN 2018019326 (print) | LCCN 2018024703 (ebook) | ISBN 9781541543003 (eb pdf) | ISBN 9781541538504 (library binding : alk. paper) | ISBN 9781541545786 (paperback : alk. paper)
Subjects: LCSH: Biles, Simone, 1997–—Juvenile literature. | Women gymnasts—United States—Biography—Juvenile literature | Gymnasts—United States—Biography—Juvenile literature.
Classification: LCC GV460.2.B55 (ebook) | LCC GV460.2.B55 F573 2019 (print) | DDC 796.44092—dc23

LC record available at https://lccn.loc.gov/2018019326

Manufactured in the United States of America
1-45033-35860-6/27/2018

Table of Contents

Gymnastics Gold 4

Gymnastics Gear 22

Picture Glossary 23

Read More 24

Index 24

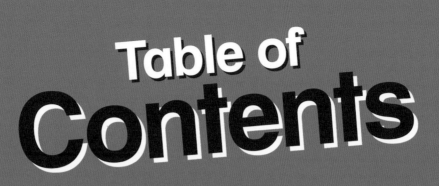

Gymnastics Gold

Simone Biles jumps and flips.

She is a superstar gymnast.

Simone loved to jump as a kid.

She jumped on the couch at home.

Her family brought her to a gym.

A coach at the gym helped

Simone become a gymnast.

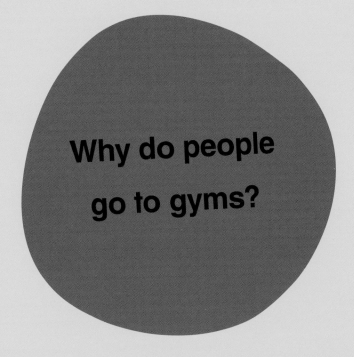

Why do people go to gyms?

Simone could flip and spin right away.

She worked hard to get even better.

She became one of the best gymnasts

in the world.

She could jump higher than other

gymnasts.

Simone went to the

Olympic Games in 2016.

She was part of the

United States team.

Simone won four gold medals at the

Olympic Games.

Why do people try to win gold medals?

The Olympic Games made Simone famous.

She appeared on lots of TV shows.

Simone still works hard in the gym.

She could win even more gold medals!

Gymnastics Gear

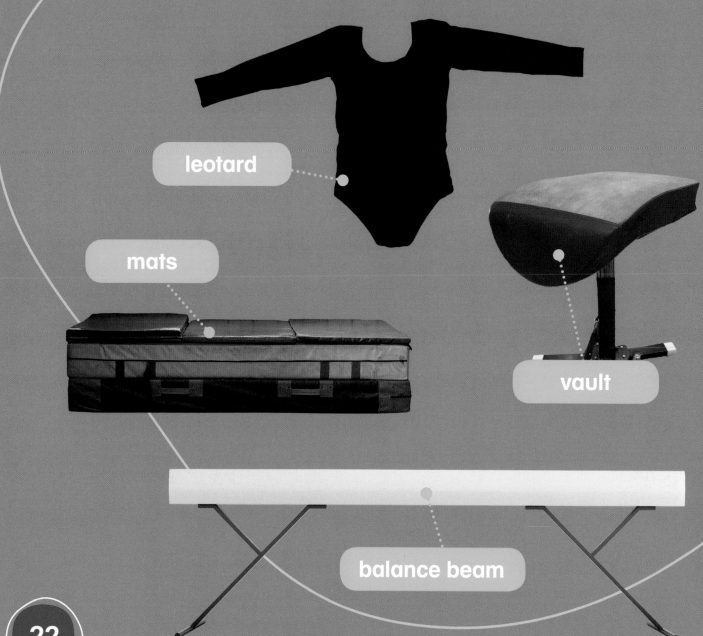

leotard

vault

mats

balance beam

Picture Glossary

coach

a person who trains athletes

gold medals

the top prize at the Olympic Games

gymnast

a person who does flips and other moves in a gym

Olympic Games

a worldwide sports contest held every two years in either winter or summer

23

Read More

Buckley, James, Jr. *Simone Biles*. New York: Bearport, 2018.

Flynn, Brendan. *Gymnastics Time!* Minneapolis: Lerner Publications, 2017.

Schuh, Mari. *Gymnastics*. Mankato, MN: Amicus, 2018.

Index

coach, 8

gold medals, 21

gym, 8, 21

Olympic Games, 15

team, 15

TV shows, 18

Photo Credits

Image credits: icons: Amy Salveson/Independent Picture Service; Tim Clayton/Corbis/Getty Images, pp. 5, 10, 14–15, 20, 23 (bottom left), 23 (bottom right); Dean Mouhtaropoulos/Getty Images, p. 6; AP Photo/ Matthias Schrader, pp. 8–9, 23 (top left); Leonard Zhukovsky/Shutterstock.com, p. 13; BEN STANSALL/AFP/ Getty Images, pp. 16, 23 (top right); Tim Warner/Getty Images, p. 19; StanislauV/Shutterstock.com, p. 22 (top); Sergiy1975/Shutterstock.com, p. 22 (middle left); Polhansen/Shutterstock.com, p. 22 (middle right); 3DMAVR/ Shutterstock.com, p. 22 (bottom).

Cover: Alex Livesey/Getty Images.